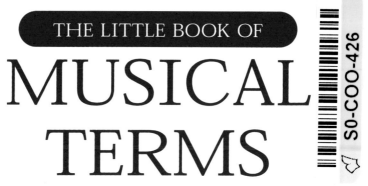

THE LITTLE BOOK OF
MUSICAL
TERMS

Your essential A–Z guide to the language of music.

Amsco Publications
New York/London/Paris/Sydney/Copenhagen/Madrid

Order No. AM 962000
US International Standard Book Number: 0.8256.1810.X
UK International Standard Book Number: 0.7119.7825.5

Exclusive Distributors:
Music Sales Corporation
257 Park Avenue South, New York, NY 10010 USA
Music Sales Limited
8/9 Frith Street, London W1D 3JB England
Music Sales Pty. Limited
120 Rothschild Street, Rosebery, Sydney, NSW 2018, Australia

Printed in the United States of America by
Vicks Lithograph and Printing Corporation

A capella
Sung by unaccompanied voices.

A tempo
Return to the original speed.

Accelerando
Gradually increase the **tempo**.
Abbreviated *accel*.

Accent
A small arrow-like mark placed on a
note or **chord** giving it more emphasis.

Acciaccatura
A note that theoretically has no duration,
added before another note as a
decoration.

Accidental
A **sharp** (♯), **flat** (♭), or **natural** (♮) sign
which raises or lowers a note by a **half
step** (or restores it to its usual pitch).

Acoustic
1. The sound characteristic of a room.
2. A term describing a musical
instrument designed for use without an
amplifier.

Action
The height of the strings from the
fretboard or neck of a stringed
instrument, notably the guitar.

Ad lib.
Improvise a section or repeat a phrase
with extemporaneous variations.

Adagio
A slow tempo; faster than **Largo,** but
slower than **Andante**.

ADT
Automatic Double Tracking. A
recording technique used to thicken a
vocal line or instrument. The part is re-
recorded onto an adjacent track with a
slightly different echo or other effect, to
create the illusion of two voices or
instruments.

Aeolian
One of seven ancient scales, the Aeolian
mode is the same as the **natural minor
scale:** A B C D E F G A.

Air
A type of melody or song that occurs
initially in French and English music of
the Renaissance. The air is traditionally
sung with lute accompaniment.

Allegro
A quick **tempo;** faster than **Moderato,**
but slower than **Presto.**

Allemande
A popular baroque dance, also known as
an *alman*, which formed part of the 16th
century suite.

Altered chord
A **chord** in which a note (or notes) has
been changed. The altered chord C7(♭5)
(C E G♭ B♭) has a flatted fifth (G♭).

Alto
A low female (or high male) vocal
range, spanning from G below **Middle
C** to the C above it.

Ambient
A term used to describe electronic music
that has a dreamy quality achieved using
reverb.

Anacrusis
An unstressed note or notes at the start
of a piece of music or musical phrase.

Andante
A moderate **tempo** or walking pace;
faster than **Adagio,** but slower than
Allegro.

Animato
Played in a lively, spirited manner.

Anticipation
Playing a note (or notes) or a chord
shortly before the remaining notes. This
technique is used to create the rhythmic
effect **syncopation** used in blues and
jazz music.

Antiphonal
An arrangement in which a piece of
music uses two groups of performers to
generate a *call-and-response* structure.

Anthem
A choral composition deriving from the
Latin motet, written for performance in
church, and usually accompanied by
organ.

AOR
Adult Oriented Rock. A type of
commercial rock music made popular in
the U.S. during the 1970s and 1980s by
such groups as Fleetwood Mac, Boston,
and Foreigner. See also **MOR.**

Appoggiatura

A **grace note** that creates a brief **dissonance** before resolving down to the next note. The appoggiatura is usually a **whole step** or half step above the main note.

Aria

A song or song-like piece, usually from an opera. Presented in three sections: A-B-A. If the middle section is omitted, an *arietta*.

Arpeggio

A figure in which the notes of a **chord** are played individually in sequence rather than simultaneously.

Atonal music

Music written without the organizing principles of established **keys, scales, and harmony**.

Augmented

A term used to describe an interval that is one half step larger than a **major** or **perfect** interval. Also used to describe a **triad** made up of two major thirds (such as C E G♯).

B

Backline

The amplifiers arranged at the back of the stage for individual musicians. The backline complements the monitor system and the **PA** (public address) system.

Backup track

Recorded music used for accompaniment, such as an instrumental mix of a song. Popularized by the widespread use of karaoke machines; backup tracks are also frequently used for televised music performances. Also called *backing track*.

Backward guitar

A recording technique popularized in the 1960s. Reels of tape are taken off a reel-to-reel tape recorder and reversed. The guitarist then records a solo in the appropriate section, starting where the solo is meant to end, and ending where the solo will start. When the tape is put back the right way, and played back, the notes are reversed.

Ballad

A song telling a story in which each verse is set to the same music. The term *ballade* describes a romantic piece for a single instrument, a form favored by composers such as Brahms and Schumann.

Bar

1. A line placed across the staff that divides music into rhythmic sections. Also called a *barline*.

2. A section of music falling between two *barlines*. Also called a *measure*.

Bar
Barline

3. A guitar fretting technique where a finger (usually the first) is laid flat on the neck to hold down more than one string. Sometimes spelled *barre*.

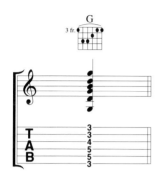

Baritone

A male vocal range of medium-low pitch, spanning from F♯ above **Middle C** down nearly two octaves to A.

Baroque

European music of the period from 1600 to 1750. Notable baroque composers include J.S. Bach, Vivaldi, Purcell, Corelli, Handel, and Scarlatti.

Bass

1. The lowest part of a musical composition, significant for stabilizing and defining the **harmony.**
2. A male vocal range, spanning from F below the bass staff to D above **Middle C.**

Bass drum

Along with the snare, the most important part of the drum kit, supplying a low frequency *thud* which is offset by the higher frequency *crack* of the snare. Most popular-music arrangements are characterized by repeating patterns using these two drums.

Bass guitar

Devised in the 1950s, the four strings of the bass guitar are tuned to the same notes as the lower four strings of the guitar (E A D G), but an octave lower. The electric bass is a vital part of the rhythm section in most popular-music arrangements.

Beatbox

An electronic drum machine used in contemporary dance music.

Bend

A smooth change in pitch (usually limited to a **half step** or **whole step**) frequently heard in blues, jazz, and rock music.

Bi-amping

A method of amplifying a signal by first splitting it into high and low frequencies, and then sending each resultant signal to its own separate power amp (which drives an appropriate speaker, or group of speakers).

Binary form
A baroque musical form with two complementary sections.

Bitonality
The use of two different **keys** at the same time.

Black notes
Notes played using the five black keys of the piano: C♯ D♯ F♯ G♯ A♯ (also called D♭ E♭ G♭ A♭ B♭).

Blue note
A note that creates the harmonic tension typical of the **blues.** The most common blue notes are the flatted third and flatted seventh.

Blues
An African-American folk music often expressing the Black experience of social oppression. The blues began as a rural music in the Mississippi Delta region, with the first recordings dating back to the 1920s. The migration of many blacks to northern cities led to the development of an urban, electric blues typified by performers such as Muddy Waters and Howlin' Wolf. The constituent parts of blues music are extremely simple. The main forms are 8, 12, 16, or 32 bars long. The harmony focuses on I7, IV7, and V7 chords. The melody exhibits the use of the flatted third, fifth, and seventh of the **scale.** These notes deliberately clash with the major tonality underneath. Blues enjoyed a significant revival in the 1960s when British rock musicians such as Eric Clapton and John Mayall introduced it to a wider audience by recording blues songs and appearing with the likes of John Lee Hooker, Howlin' Wolf, and B.B. King.

Bolero
A type of Spanish dance in triple time (now forever associated with the languid modal **melody** and surging rhythms of Ravel's composition of this name and "Beck's Bolero" by guitarists Jeff Beck and Jimmy Page).

Boogie-woogie
A type of rhythmic **blues** popular in the 1940s and 1950s, chiefly for piano. The player's right hand is free to improvise phrases, while the left hand maintains steady, repeating **bass** figures.

Bootleg

An unofficial recording (usually of a concert) circulated in cassette, vinyl, or CD format. Despite their illegality, the legendary status of bootlegs has done much to stimulate interest in major performers and to sustain their presence in popular music long after the act in question has split up. Possibly the most famous bootleg of all time was a recording of Bob Dylan's 1966 concert at the Manchester Free Trade Hall, entitled *Live at the Royal Albert Hall.*

Bottleneck

Metal or glass tube placed on the third or fourth finger of the fretting hand, used by guitarists to produce distinctive **glissando** and **vibrato** effects. Altered tunings often assist the **slide** technique, which is heard in **blues**, rock, and folk music.

Bouncing

A technique by which a recording is re-recorded onto another track, sometimes as another part is added. Bounces can be single (track 1 to track 2) or multiple (tracks 1–7 onto 8). Also known as *ping-ponging.*

Bourée

A type of French dance similar to the **gavotte** but taken at a quicker **tempo** in ⁴ time, and starting on the last beat of the **measure.**

BPM

Beats Per Minute. A standard measure of tempo indicated by a note and number (*e.g.,* ♩ = 120).

Bridge

1. A transitional section in a song connecting the **verse** and **chorus.**
2. In instruments like the guitar and violin, the piece of wood or metal over which the strings pass to the neck.

Broken chord

An accompaniment style in which the **chords** are split up. Often the root note is played first, followed by the third and fifth together.

Bossa nova

A popular Brazilian dance music characterized by syncopation.

C

Cadence
A **chord** pattern that marks the end of a phrase in traditional **harmony.** There are four main types of cadence: **perfect, imperfect, plagal,** and **interrupted.**

Cadenza
A passage that occurs toward the conclusion of a **concerto** movement designed to exhibit the technical brilliance of the featured soloist.

Calypso
A dance and song form with its origins in West Indian folk music, associated with Trinidad and the Caribbean.

Canon
Music in which several voices sing the same melodic line but begin and end at different times. Unlike a **round,** the second voice can enter before the first has finished its phrase, and may be transposed down or up a fourth or fifth.

Cantabile
In a singing style.

Cantata
A piece of music composed for solo voices, **chorus,** and **orchestra.** During the **baroque** era, it was a sacred work.

Eventually the cantata also developed secular themes.

Capo
A device that wraps around the neck of a fretted instrument, raising the pitch of the strings. The capo is often used by guitarists to play in difficult **keys,** or in keys that suit a singer's voice. This useful device also changes the tone of the guitar, making unique **chord** voicings possible high up the neck.

Catch
A tune with three or four phrases that can be sung simultaneously. The catch is started one phrase at a time until all parts are going. Examples include "London's Burning" and "Frère Jacques."

Chamber music
Music written for intimate surroundings rather than the concert hall. The **string quartet** is a typical chamber ensemble.

Chorale
A type of hymn tune, most notably associated with J.S. Bach. Generations of students have learned **harmony** by analyzing the **chords** of Bach chorales.

Chord

A group of more than two notes played together (in contrast to an **interval,** which consists of only two notes).

Chorus

1. In **classical** music, a group of singers supplying vocal sections in a longer work.
2. The most memorable section of a song, usually repeated.
3. An electronic **delay** effect that slightly alters the pitch of the original signal and thickens the overall sound.

Chromatic

A term that refers to a note that does not normally occur within the **key.** Thus in C major, the notes C♯, D♯, F♯, G♯, and A♯ are all chromatic notes.
Chromaticism is the extensive use of such notes to extend the **harmony.**

Circle of fifths

A progression of the **keys** depicted in a circle. Starting at C major, the major **keys** progress by fifths: G, D, A, E, B, F♯, D♭, A♭, E♭, B♭, F, and finally C, thus completing the circle.

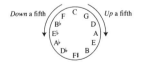

Classical

European music of the mid eighteenth to early nineteenth century typified by Mozart and Haydn. Music from the classical period has a well-defined **harmony** and a strong commitment to formal rules of composition.

Clef

A sign placed on the **staff** to fix the pitches of the lines and spaces. The G treble clef fixes the second line as G, the F bass clef fixes the fourth line as F. There are also C alto clefs and tenor clefs.

Treble clef   Alto clef   Bass clef

Click bass

A popular electric bass style of the late 1960s and early 1970s defined by a trebly tone and the use of a pick. This distinctive playing style imitates the eighth-note **syncopation** of the **Motown** bassist James Jamerson.

Coda

The final section of a piece of music.

Compact disc

A digital recording format. Information stored on a *CD* is read by a laser.

Common time

Another term for $\frac{4}{4}$ time which features four quarter-note beats in a bar.

Camping

Providing a simple chordal accompaniment to a soloist. Also known as *vamping*.

Compound interval

The distance between two notes that are more than an **octave** apart. A major ninth is the compound version of a major second.

Major 2nd   Major 9th

Compound time

A time signature in which each pulse consists of a dotted note or its equivalent. (*e.g.*, $\frac{6}{8}$, $\frac{9}{8}$, or $\frac{12}{8}$). See also **simple time.**

Compression

A type of signal processing used in recordings to increase the volume of quieter sounds and limit louder ones. This prevents peak signals which would otherwise flaw the recording.

Concerto

A large-scale concert work in three movements, usually for **orchestra** and a solo instrument.

Consonance

Combinations of notes that are pleasing to the ear. See also **dissonance.**

Contrary motion

An effect created when two melodic lines move in opposite directions. This contrasts with *oblique motion*, where one voice remains on the same note while the other moves, or **parallel motion,** in which both voices move in the same direction.

Counterpoint

The combination of two or more melodic lines that move independently of each other, yet still sustain a sense of harmonic organization. Counterpoint is typically heard in music of the classical and pre-classical eras.

Countertenor

The highest male voice, not to be confused with male **alto** or **falsetto.**

Crescendo

A direction used to indicate an increase in volume.

Crosstalk

An unwanted sound heard on analog **multitrack** recordings. Because of the existence of parallel tracks on tape, some of the signal on one track can be heard on an adjacent track at high volume or during very quiet passages.

Gibson Les Paul with Single Cutaway

Cutaway

A contour of the guitar body which makes notes on the high frets more easily accessible. The Gibson Les Paul is a single cutaway guitar. The Fender Stratocaster is a double cutaway.

Fender Stratocaster with Double Cutaway

D

DAT
Digital Audio Tape. Trademarked name for a type of audio tape on which digital information can be stored in two tracks.

D.C. al fine
Abbreviation for *da capo al fine*. A music direction indicating the performer should return to the beginning of a piece and play through until reaching the word *fine*.

Decibel
A unit for measuring relative levels of power, voltage, and sound intensity, and hence an objective indication of loudness. Abbreviated *dB*.

Delay
An effect originally called *echo*. Here, a note or sound is recorded and then played back repeatedly, usually at progressively softer volumes.

Demo
A demonstration recording made by an artist or songwriter, and not intended for release. A demo is usually used to attract the interest of music publishers, club owners, agents, or production companies.

Development
A composing technique in **classical** music whereby the initial musical statement (the **exposition**) is extended and changed. Development is essential to longer works such as **sonatas, concertos,** and **symphonies.**

Diatonic
Derived from the notes of the standard major or minor scale. See also **chromatic.**

Diminished
A term used to describe an interval that is one half-step smaller than a **major** or **perfect** interval. Also used to describe a **triad** made up of two minor thirds (such as C E♭ G♭).
If another minor third is added (B♭♭ or A), the *diminished seventh chord* is formed. The diminished **triad** naturally occurs as the VII chord in a major **key** (in C major, B D F).

Diminuendo
A direction used to indicate a decrease in volume.

Dirge

A general term for any slow piece of a mournful nature, especially connected with a funeral.

Disco

A style of dance music popular in the 1970s and celebrated in the film *Saturday Night Fever*. Disco is typified by a four-to-the-bar bass drum beat with pronounced eighth-note octaves in the bass.

Dissonance

An unharmonious sound used to create tension in music. The minor second (C-C♯), augmented fourth (C-F♯), and major seventh (C-B) are dissonant intervals.

C-B

Dominant

The fifth note and **chord** of the **scale**.

Dominant Chord

Dorian

One of seven ancient scales, the Dorian **mode** is a **natural minor scale** with a raised sixth: D E F G A B C D.

D   E   F   G   A   B   C   D

Dot

Placed after a note, the dot increases the duration of that note by one-half. Thus, a dotted **quarter note** lasts for one-and-one-half beats. Similarly, a double dot increases the duration of the note by one-half plus a quarter. Thus a double-dotted **half note** lasts for three-and-one-half beats.

Downbeat

The first beat of a **measure** (in ⁴⁄₄ time, also the third beat). Downbeats contrast with upbeats, which occur on beats two and four. See also **upbeat.**

Drone

A note or group of notes either sustained or played repeatedly to complement a **melody** or changing **chords.**

Dry

A term used to describe a sound signal without any effects processing (such as **reverb**). Opposite of **wet.**

D.S. al fine

Abbreviation for *dal segno al fine*. A music direction indicating the performer should return to the *dal segno sign* (𝄋) and play through until reaching the word *fine*.

Dynamics

Degrees of volume in a musical work.

p = soft (piano)

mf = moderately loud (mezzo forte)

f = loud (forte)

Early music
A term that describes Western music composed before or during the Renaissance. Generally this refers to music composed up to about 1650. In recent times, it has become popular to play this music with the greatest possible authenticity. This is accomplished using reproductions of antique instruments and avoiding any performance techniques that were the product of later centuries of musical development.

E-bow
A battery-powered device held in a guitarist's picking hand which causes the string to produce an endlessly sustained note.

Effects unit
An analog or digital device designed to modify sound. These range from small, single-effect units that are turned on and off with footswitches to complex multi-parameter programmable modules. Effects units may be used with most electric instruments. When used as part of the recording/mixing process, an effects unit can also alter the sound of **acoustic** instruments.

Eighth note
A note with half the duration of a **quarter note.** In most circumstances, the eighth note lasts for one-half of a beat.

Electric guitar
A version of the classical (Spanish) and steel-string acoustic instrument that relies on magnetic **pickups** for much of its sound. The vibrating strings create fluctuations in the magnetic field, which in turn are converted into an electric signal. This signal is then strengthened by an amplifier and made audible through a speaker. The electric guitar may be solid, semihollow, or hollow-bodied. It is tuned in the same manner as the **acoustic** guitar, although it tends to be strung with lighter gauge strings. Very few instruments have the potential to move as much air and generate as much sound as the electric guitar. Marketed at first as a novelty, the electric guitar is among the most popular instruments of the twentieth century.

Electro-acoustic guitar
A type of **acoustic** guitar developed in the 1970s with a built-in amplification system. This instrument has a built-in **pickup** and tone/volume controls which allow the sound to pass directly to an amplifier or **PA** system. The first models were steel-string, but recently nylon-string examples have appeared on the market.

Enharmonic

A term used to described tones of
virtually the same **pitch** that are derived
from different degrees of the **scale** (and
have different names). For example, C♯
and D♭ are enharmonic tones.
Enharmonic chords are those that
contain the same pitches, but are notated
differently.

Enhancer

A sound processing device that adds an
overall sparkle to the **mix** or gives one
instrument greater prominence.

Equalization

A mixing process used during a
recording or live perfomance in which
selected **frequencies** can be cut or
boosted to enhance the tonal balance.
Abbreviated *EQ*.

Etude

A musical piece of variable form
designed to allow the performer or
student to explore particular technical
skills.

Exposition

The initial statement of a musical theme
(which is then subject to **development**).

Fader
A sliding control on a mixing console that increases or reduces the level of the signal.

Falsetto
A technique used by male vocalists to extend the upward range of their voices. The falsetto voice uses only part of the vocal chords, and is therefore weaker than the normal voice.

Fanfare
A short, showy piece of music, usually played on brass instruments at a ceremonial occasion.

Feedback
Noise created when an amplified sound is fed back into the electrical system that produced it. This causes the sound to sustain, increase in volume, and often decay into one of its higher **harmonics.**

Flam
A technique used by drummers in which the snare drum is struck by both sticks a fraction of a second apart, creating a dramatic effect.

Flamenco
A traditional dance music of Spain, featuring a **virtuoso** guitar technique combining vigorous strumming, percussive tapping of the guitar body, and **Phrygian** melodies.

Figured bass
A system of **notation** in which numbers written in the **bass** line indicate the **chords** to be used. Usually associated with baroque keyboard accompaniments.

Finale
The last movement of a longer piece of music with several movements.

Fine
A musical direction indicating the end of a composition.

Fingering
1. A system of marks (usually numbers) indicating which fingers to use when playing a piece.
2. An interpretive process in which an instrumentalist chooses which fingers to use to play each note in a piece in order to produce the best performance.

Flanging
A sound effect created with **electric guitar** involving a moving sweep of **frequencies.**

Flat
A sign placed in front of a note, lowering it by a **half step.** A type of **accidental.** See also **sharp** and **natural.**

B   B flat

Foldback
See **monitor.**

Folk baroque
A term coined to describe the ornate fingerstyle of 1960s folk guitarists such as John Renbourn, Bert Jansch, and Davey Graham.

Folk music
Traditional song or dance music, usually associated with a particular culture or nation. True folk music has no known composer and is handed down by oral tradition. However many songs composed in the folk style (especially during the 1960s) are also commonly included in this category.

Folk rock
A hybrid of Anglo-American **folk music** developed in the 1960s. In this style, traditional material is arranged for a **rock** ensemble (usually including **acoustic** guitar, **electric guitar, bass,** drums, and sometimes mandolin or **violin**).

Forte
A musical direction indicating the performer should play loudly. Usually notated with the symbol f. See also **dynamics.**

Fortepiano
A successor to the harpsichord and forerunner of the modern piano; popular during the eighteenth century.

Frequency
The pitch of a note, as measured by the number of cycles per second. One *Hertz* equals one cycle per second. **Middle C** is 256 Hertz. Abbreviated *Hz.*

Fret
A thin piece of metal, wood, or ivory that is hammered into the fingerboard of a guitar (or other fretted instrument). The fret marks the place where the finger is placed to produce a note.

Fretless bass
A type of electric **bass guitar** made without frets to facilitate smooth glissandos and similar expressive effects. This instrument was popularized by Jaco Pastorius in the 1970s.

Fugue
A complex **baroque** work usually composed for keyboard and involving the statement and **development** of musical themes that overlap in a precise manner. The most famous examples are the *Preludes and Fugues* composed by J.S. Bach.

Fundamental
1. The primary tone or *root* of a chord.
2. A note that produces **harmonics.**

Funk
A commercial African-American music developed from rhythm and blues by James Brown in the 1960s and popularized in the 1970s. This is an earthy form of soul music with strong bass and syncopated rhythms, often featuring a strong emphasis on the first beat of each measure.

FX
An abbreviation for *sound effects*.

G

Gain

A control on a mixing console, amplifier, or signal processor that increases the input level on a particular channel. On guitar amplifiers, the gain control increases distortion.

Galliard

A lively dance of the sixteenth century, usually in ⅜ time.

Garage band

1. A nonprofessional **rock** band, usually characterized by a simple, rough style. The term is derived from the fact that many amateur bands in the 1960s had limited resources and practiced in the garage.
2. A term used to describe the primitive style of music typical of nonprofessional rock bands.

Gavotte

A French dance of the eighteenth century in ⅜ time featuring a lively **tempo** and four-bar phrases that often start in the middle of the **bar**.

Gig

A colloquial expression for a professional or semiprofessional concert or live performance, usually featuring **rock** or **jazz** musicians.

Giusto

Also *tempo giusto*. A tempo direction indicating a piece should be played with a strict **tempo.**

Glam rock

A form of **rock** music popularized in England from 1971 to 1974 by David Bowie, T. Rex, and Roxy Music. Glam rejected the musical pretensions of **progressive rock** and revived some musical traits of the rock music of the 1950s.

Glissando

An ascending or descending progression of notes in a continuous sequence.

Grace note

A short, ornamental note added to a regular note to create musical interest. See also **acciaccatura** and **appoggiatura**.

Gospel

An influential style of African-American vocal music originally sung during church services with clapping, but little or no instrumental accompaniment. The vocal style is **blues**-influenced, features call-and-response forms, and allows for individual voices to decorate short phrases at will. Gospel music was a vital part of the development of **soul music** in the 1960s as popularized by Aretha Franklin.

Graphic equalizer
A sound processing device that enables
very fine adjustments to be made to
different frequencies, which are divided
into *bands*.

Gregorian chant
An early form of Western sacred vocal
music named after Pope Gregory
(590–604) utilizing unaccompanied
unison singing in a flowing metre
without accents.

Groove
A slang term used to refer to the subtler
aspects of **rhythm** in a popular song or
instrumental piece. This term refers to
the overall *feel* of a rhythm, which is
usually characterized by slight
anticipations and delays of different
beats.

Grunge
A style of **rock** music that enjoyed
considerable success in the early 1990s,
arising from the Seattle music scene and
exemplified by the band Nirvana.
Grunge took the **riffs** of **hard rock** and
combined these with the anarchic
mentality of **punk** to create a revolution
in rock music.

Half note

A note with half the duration of a **whole note.** In most circumstances, the half note lasts for two beats.

1 - 2   1 - 2

Half step

The smallest **interval** in conventional Western music. Also called a *minor second* or *semitone*. There are twelve half-steps in an **octave.**

Hard rock

A style of **rock** music that developed from the blues-rock music of the late 1960s. Songs feature repeated guitar figures played at a low pitch (and usually based on **pentatonic** minor and **blues** scales). High volume levels, powerful drumming, and extended guitar solos inspired vocalists to pitch ever higher in an effort to be heard. Legendary hard rock bands include Led Zeppelin, Deep Purple, and Black Sabbath.

Harmonic minor scale

A scale created when the seventh degree of the **natural minor scale** is raised by one half-step: A B C D E F G♯ A. See

also **melodic minor scale, minor scale,** and **natural minor scale.**

Harmonics

1. A series of **overtones** that sound above the **fundamental** tone at fixed intervals and form part of the overall **timbre** of the sound.
2. Overtones played on stringed instruments by lightly touching a string at specific points.

Harmony

The underlying **chord** structure of a piece of music, usually based in a chosen **key** or mixture of keys.

Harmonization

The process of adding **chords** to a melody.

Heavy metal

A style of **rock** music popularized in the 1980s that evolved from the **hard rock** of the 1960s. This style features a heavy, repetitive beat and low-pitched guitar **riffs.** It is often characterized by extensive guitar solos, **tritones,** and morbid **lyrics** focusing on death and destruction. Heavy metal music is exemplified by such bands as Iron Maiden, AC/DC, and Metallica.

Hi-hat

An essential component of the contemporary drum set, this instrument has two matching cymbals that can be opened and closed using a foot pedal and hit with a drumstick. The hi-hat is an important timekeeper in **rock** and **jazz** music, and is often used to generate a continuous stream of **eighth notes.**

Hip-hop
A form of African-American music that developed from the club culture of New York City in the late 1980s. The disk jockey becomes an instrumentalist who plays a multideck turntable by manipulating vinyl records (a technique called *scratching*). Today, drum **loops, rapping,** and improvisation are also important elements of this popular dance music.

Hook
The line of a song most likely to imprint itself on a listener after hearing it once or twice. Often repeated, the hook is also commonly reflected in the song's title.

Humbucker
A type of electric guitar **pickup** that was developed in the 1950s. This device has two magnetic coils which help "buck the hum" endemic to single-coil pickups. Humbuckers are quieter than single coils and have a thicker, less trebly tone.

Hungarian scale
The harmonic minor scale with an augmented fourth. In the Key of C: C D E♭ F♯ G A♭ B C. The presence of minor third leaps (E♭ to F♯ and A♭ to B) gives this scale an exotic sound.

C   D   E♭   F♯   G   A♭   B   C

I

Imperfect cadence

The progression of **chords** I to V at the end of a musical phrase, creating a feeling of expectancy.

I - V
C   D

Impromptu

A musical piece with an informal structure and impulsive style favored by nineteenth-century composers such as Schumann, Chopin, Mendelssohn, and Liszt.

Intelligent

A term used to describe effects devices, especially harmonizers, that are able to imitate certain musical processes.

Intonation

1. The production of a musical tone.
2. Singing or playing in tune.

Interrupted cadence

The movement of the V chord to a chord other than I (usually the VI chord) at the end of a musical phrase.

V   VI
D   Em

Interval

The distance between two notes. The intervals of the **major scale** are: major second, major third, perfect fourth, perfect fifth, major sixth, major seventh, and **octave.**

C major

M2   M3   P4

P5   M6   M7   Octave

Inversion

The transposition of the notes of a **chord** in **root position.** In the key of C minor, the root position is C E♭ G. The *first inversion* features the E♭ note in the bass. The *second inversion* features the G note in the bass.

C minor

Root   1st   2nd
        inversion   inversion

Ionian
One of seven ancient scales, the Ionian
mode is the same as the **major scale:**
C D E F G A B C.

IPS
Inches Per Second. A standard measure
of speed for analog tape recorders.

J

Jam
A term used to describe the playing of improvisational music by a **jazz** or **rock** ensemble.

Jangle guitar
A style of **electric guitar** playing used in pop and **rock** music. Characterized by arpeggiation, this rhythmic style exploits the guitar's ability to produce chord voicings that include more than one note of the same pitch. Jangle guitar playing was popularized by George Harrison of the Beatles and Roger McGuinn of the Byrds, both of whom played the Rickenbacker electric twelve-string guitar.

Jazz
A popular African-American music with roots in the **blues.** Beginning in New Orleans during the 1920s, this important musical genre includes a range of subgenres: ragtime, Dixieland, swing, bebop, free-form, avant-garde, as well as hybrids such as jazz-funk and **jazz-rock**. Jazz music often has complex **harmony,** and uses **swing rhythm** and **blue notes**. This genre usually focuses on **development** more than other popular forms, particularly through improvisation.

Jazz-rock
A fusion of **jazz** and **rock** styles initiated in the 1960s. Notable pioneers of this style include Miles Davis, Herbie Hancock, and Keith Jarrett.

Jingle
A catchy, short piece of instrumental or vocal music used to advertise a product or service.

Jug band
A **folk music** ensemble that incorporates homemade or found instruments such as the jug, washboard, washtub bass, and spoons. These are usually accompanied by traditional instruments such as the **acoustic** guitar and harmonica to produce simple, rhythmic folk music.

Jumbo
A term applied to an extra large-bodied acoustic guitar. The most famous model is Gibson's J-200, which was designed in the late 1930s.

Jungle
An outgrowth of **hip-hop,** this subgenre of 1990s dance music is played on electronic keyboards and drum machines, and features a primitive rhythmic sound.

Key

A sense of tonality which governs music and is based on a major or **minor scale.** For example, the C **major scale** features the notes C D E F G A B C and generates the **chords** C Dm Em F G Am, Bdim. A composition in the Key of C Major creates a sense of key in which the tonic note C and the **tonic chord** (C E G) provide a center around which the rest of the piece is organized. There is an aesthetic pleasure each time the tonic chord is reached and an awareness of journeying away from it when the **harmony** moves to other chords.

Key signature

An arrangement of accidentals at the beginning of a piece indicating the key. There are fifteen key signatures: seven **sharp,** seven **flat,** and C major which has no sharps or flats.

Kick drum

A Major   B♭ Major

See **bass drum.**

Koto

A Japanese stringed instrument, resembling a **zither,** with thirteen strings; may be tuned to various **pentatonic** scales.

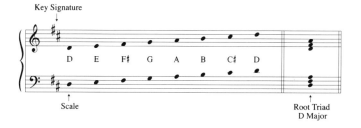

Key Signature

D E F♯ G A B C♯ D

Scale

Root Triad
D Major

L

Largo
The slowest **tempo,** usually executed in a broad and stately manner.

Lead guitar
In pop and **rock** music, the guitar part that complements the vocal **melody** and provides solos. Usually played on an **electric guitar,** the lead guitar style was refined in the 1960s by such artists as Eric Clapton, Jeff Beck, Jimmy Page, Jimi Hendrix, Carlos Santana, and many others.

Leading tone
The seventh note of the scale. In many scales, this tone is one half-step below the tonic note.

Leakage
The intrusion of one instrument's sound into the microphone of another instrument.

Legato
A musical direction indicating the performer should play smoothly.

Leger line
A small line added to a note written above or below the staff that makes it easier to read. Also sometimes *ledger line.*

Leitmotiv
The *leading motive;* a distinctive musical phrase in a longer dramatic work that characterizes a particular character or concept. Often occurring in operas, notably those by Wagner.

Leslie effect
A sound created by feeding a signal through a *Leslie speaker* revolving at a high speed to create fluctuations in pitch. This effect is most commonly used with keyboard or guitar. The **bridge** section of Cream's "Badge" illustrates the sound of a guitar processed using this effect.

Libretto
The words for an opera, musical, or oratorio, often printed in booklet form for the audience to read during the performance.

Lick
See **riff.**

Liturgy
The text of a Christian service set to music.

Locrian
One of seven ancient scales, the Locrian **mode** is a **natural minor scale** with a flatted second and fifth: B C D E F G A B.

Loop
Originally, a section of tape with its
ends spliced together so that it would
repeat a sound over and over when
played. In the 1960s, the Beatles
experimented with tape loops in songs
like "Tomorrow Never Knows" and
"Being for the Benefit of Mr. Kite."
Today, looping is achieved using digital
sampling.

Lullaby
A cradle song.

Lute
A forerunner of the guitar that was
popular throughout Europe from the
Middle Ages through the eighteenth
century. The number of strings and the
body dimensions varied greatly from
instrument to instrument, but common
features included a curved-back body,
sound holes, catgut frets, and strings
doubled at the same pitch. In the 1590s,
composers such as John Dowland
developed a complex, contrapuntal style
for this instrument.

Lydian
One of seven ancient scales, the Lydian
mode is a **major scale** with a raised
fourth: F G A B C D E F.

F   G   A   B   C   D   E   F

Lyric
The words to a song. Also sometimes
lyrics.

Lyrical
Sung or played in a melodious manner.

M

Madrigal
An Italian song form popular throughout Europe before and during the Renaissance. The madrigal is usually sung by a small group of unaccompanied voices in counterpoint and features secular themes.

Maestoso
A musical direction indicating the performer should play majestically.

Mainstream
A term applied to contemporary music that has wide popular appeal.

Major scale
A pattern of notes arranged in a fixed interval sequence: whole step, whole step, half step, whole step, whole step, whole step, half step.

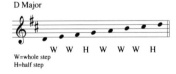

D Major

W W H W W W H
W=whole step
H=half step

Measure
See **bar (2)**.

Mediant
The third note of a scale.

Medley
An arrangement that combines extracts from two or more compositions into a single continuous performance.

Melisma
1. A group of notes sung to a single syllable.
2. The decoration of a melody by a singer to intensify the emotional impact of a song. This technique is common in **soul, rhythm and blues,** and **gospel.**

Melody
A sequence of single notes which form the primary focus of interest in a musical piece.

Melodic minor scale
A scale created when the sixth and seventh degrees of the **natural minor scale** are raised by one half-step during ascending musical passages. Ascending: A B C D E F♯ G♯ A. Descending: A G♮ F♮ E D C B A. See also **harmonic minor scale, minor scale,** and **natural minor scale.**

C minor

Mellotron
A keyboard designed during the 1960s to imitate strings, flutes, and other orchestral instruments. Physically heavy and subject to tuning problems, the Mellotron has long since been superseded by digital samplers and

synthesizers, but retains a reedy charm apparent on the Beatles' "Strawberry Fields Forever" and "Nights in White Satin" by the Moody Blues.

Metronome
A mechanical or electronic device used to create a regular rhythmic pulse at any **tempo,** enabling the player to practice with a steady beat.

Microtone
An **interval** of less than a half step. Microtones commonly occur in non-Western music, as well as some avant-garde **classical** and **rock** music.

Middle C
A note with a frequency of 256 Hertz, often used as a point of reference as it is in the middle of the piano keyboard.

Middle eight
A section of a song that comes after the second **chorus** and acts as a **bridge** to a solo, a **verse,** or another **chorus.** This section is typically eight **bars** long.

MIDI
Musical Instrument Digital Interface. A software-based protocol that enables digital instruments to exchange musical information.

Minor scale
In minor keys, the third degree of the scale is an interval of a minor third (or one-and-a-half steps) from the root tone of the scale. See also **harmonic minor scale, melodic minor scale,** and **natural minor scale.**

Minuet
An early dance form in triple time developed in France and popular throughout Europe during the seventeenth and eighteenth centuries.

Mix
1. The process by which the parts of a multitrack recording are balanced and additional effects are added.
2. The final recording resulting from the mixing process.
3. The balance of instruments coming through the **PA** system during a live performance.

Mixolydian

One of seven ancient scales, the Mixolydian **mode** is a **major scale** with a flatted seventh: G A B C D E F G. Since **blues** music commonly uses a flatted seventh, the Mixolydian scale is often used in blues-influenced **rock** and pop music.

G   A   B   C   D   E   F   G

Mode

A tonal quality derived from a particular type of scale. See **Aeolian, Dorian, Ionian, Locrian, Lydian, Mixolydian,** and **Phrygian.**

Moderato

A medium tempo; faster than **Andante,** but slower than **Allegro.**

Modulation

The transition from one key or mode into another. Modulation is used to create emotional contrast in a piece as the listener is moved from one tonal center to another. To prevent monotony, modulation is an essential feature of longer musical works.

Monitor

An arrangement of speakers at the front and side of a stage that projects sound back to the performers, enabling them to hear themselves. Also called a *foldback.*

MOR

Middle of the Road. A term for commercial music popular with **mainstream** listeners. Conservative and sentimental, this type of music does not feature any rhythmic or harmonic element that is particularly innovative or stimulating. See also **AOR.**

Motown

A form of **soul music** originally released on the Motown record label, based in Detroit, from 1960 to 1972. This popular African-American dance music often featured a four-to-the-bar snare drum part to create a strong overall rhythm.

Multitrack

A type of analog or digital recording in which individual musical parts are recorded on discrete *tracks.* During the early 1960s, multitrack recording was usually limited to two, three, or four tracks. During the late 1960s, eight-track became the norm. Since then, multitrack recording has evolved to include 16, 24, 32, and even 48 tracks.

Musique concrète

A form of twentieth-century experimental music developed by French sound engineers and radio men. This esoteric musical style incorporated both musical and nonmusical sounds in an audio collage.

Mute

A technique whereby the normal sound
of an instrument is damped to create a
less forceful sound. As examples, a
trumpet is muted using a hand-held plug
which covers the bell—and a guitar is
muted by putting the side of the picking
hand on the strings near the instrument's
bridge or tailpiece.

Nashville tuning

A guitar tuning in which the lower four strings (E A D G) are replaced with thin strings so that they may be tuned an **octave** higher. A guitar thus tuned is said to be *highstrung*.

Natural

A sign placed in front of a note that cancels the effect of a **sharp** or **flat**. A type of **accidental.**

Natural minor scale

A sequence of notes arranged in a fixed interval sequence: whole step, half step, whole step, whole step, half step, whole step, whole step. Like all minor scales, the third degree of this scale is an interval of a minor third (or one-and-a-half steps) from the root tone of the scale. See also **harmonic minor scale, melodic minor scale,** and **minor scale.**

New age music

A contemporary musical style pioneered by Brian Eno. This form is intended to soothe and uplift the spirit of the listener by inducing a tranquil, quiet mood. New age music employs synthesized voices, imitations of ethnic instruments, string sounds, and special effects (such as **reverb**) to create pleasing melodies and harmonies. Often elements of **folk music** are combined with electronic music to create a contemplative and calming atmosphere.

New romantic

A subgenre of popular music developed during the 1980s. New romantic songs were typically short and catchy, and featured drum machines and synthesizers. This style was popularized by such artists as Soft Cell, Spandau Ballet, Duran Duran, the Human League, and Gary Numan.

New wave

An outgrowth of the punk-rock music of the 1970s, new wave softened some of the hard edges to create a more **mainstream** musical style. Unlike **new romantic** music, new wave frequently features the **electric guitar.** This form was popularized by such artists as Elvis Costello, the Police, Talking Heads, and the Pretenders.

Nickelodeon

A predecessor of the jukebox, this coin-operated mechanical device provided music in public areas. Like a player piano, the nickelodeon produced music by reading a perforated roll of paper. Some nickelodeons were quite elaborate and included a complete mechanical band.

Nocturne
A piece with an informal structure and dreamy style, popularized by Chopin in the nineteenth century.

Noise gate
A sound processing device that automatically silences (*gates*) a channel when the incoming signal drops below a certain volume. This prevents unwanted background noise during a performance or recording.

Notation
Any method for writing music on paper. Standard music notation features a five-line **staff.** Some instruments, such as guitar and drums, have their own form of notation. See also **tablature.**

Octave

The distance between any note and the same note twelve half-steps higher or

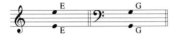

lower.

Octet

A composition for eight instruments.

Offbeat

In a bar of $\frac{4}{4}$ time, the offbeats fall after each of the beats: 1 *and* 2 *and* 3 *and* 4 *and*. **Reggae** music typically emphasizes the offbeats.

Open string

A string on an instrument such as a guitar or violin that is played without being fretted or stopped. Notes played on open strings have a distinctively rich sound quality.

Open tuning

A guitar tuning method whereby standard tuning (E A D G B E) is altered so that the open strings will produce a major or minor **chord.** *Open D* is tuned D A D F♯ A D. *Open G* is tuned D G D G B D. D A D G A D is another

common open tuning which doesn't produce a simple **triad.** Open tunings are popular among **folk** and **blues** fingerstyle and **bottleneck** players, and have even been used in a **rock** context by artists such as Jimmy Page and Keith Richards.

Opera

A large scale dramatic work for singers and **orchestra.** See also **aria** and **recitative.**

Opus

This term is followed by a number to catalog the musical work of a composer. The opus numbers usually indicate the chronology of the composer's works. For example, Beethoven's *Thirty-three Variations on a Waltz by Diabelli, Opus 120.*

Oratorio

An extended work for voices and instrumental ensemble, usually featuring a sacred theme.

Orchestra

A large ensemble of musicians playing instruments including strings, brass, woodwind, keyboard, and percussion. See also **opera, oratorio,** and **symphony.**

Orchestration

The arrangement of music for performance by an orchestra.

Ornaments
Musical embellishments used to
enhance a composition or performance.
See also **grace note, acciaccatura,** and
appoggiatura.

Ostinato
A repeated musical figure, often used in
the **bass.**

Overtones
See **harmonics.**

Overture
A piece of music originally intended as
the introduction to a longer work, often
in **medley** form.

P

PA

An abbreviation for *public address system,* the main amplification system used at a concert or other event. This system normally includes microphones, amplifiers, and speakers. During a concert, the final **mix** of onstage instrumental and vocal parts is sent to the PA for amplification. See also **monitor** and **backline.**

Pad

An unobtrusive harmonic background, performed by voices, instruments, or **synthesizer.** Also used to denote a particular sound that is appropriate for this use.

Pan

To cause a sound to seem to move to the left or right of the stereo image while mixing. Late 1960s pop-rock recordings often used panning to infuse a quality of motion, as can be heard in the **coda** to Jimi Hendrix's "House Burning Down."

Parallel motion

An effect created when two melodic lines move in the same direction. This contrasts with **contrary motion,** where the voices move in opposite directions, or *oblique motion*, where one voice

remains on the same note while the other moves.

Passing tone

A note that links two chords together, but does not actually occur in either chord. For example, a C note could serve as a passing tone between a D chord and G chord.

passing tone

Pedal tone

A repeated or sustained note that occurs beneath changing chords. Also sometimes called *pedal note* or *pedal point.*

Pentatonic

A term that describes a five-note scale, originally derived from Eastern music. Much **lead guitar** soloing in **rock** and **blues** music uses either the pentatonic minor or major. In the Key of A Minor, the pentatonic minor scale notes are A C D E G. In the key of A, the pentatonic major scale notes are A B C♯ E F♯.

Minor, in A

Major, in A

Perfect cadence

The progression of **chords** V7 to I at the end of a musical phrase, creating a feeling of finality. This is the most common type of **cadence** in Western music.

	D	D7	G
	V	V7	I

Phrasing

1. A system of marks used to indicate the expression of a musical piece.
2. An interpretive process by which a performer determines the expressions used to play or sing a particular piece.

Phrygian

One of seven ancient scales, the Phrygian **mode** is a **natural minor scale** with a lowered second: E F G A B C D E.

E F G A B C D E

Piano

1. A keyboard instrument.
2. A musical direction indicating the performer should play softly. Usually notated with the symbol **p**. See also **dynamics.**

Piano reduction

A condensed arrangement of a musical piece originally written for an ensemble into a single piano part.

Pick

1. A small piece of plastic used to strike the string of a fretted instrument. Picks come in a variety of shapes, sizes, and thicknesses. Also called a *plectrum*.
2. To pluck the strings of a fretted instrument.

Pickup

A device used to convert the sound of an **acoustic** instrument to an electric signal that can then be amplified. See also **humbucker.**

Pizzicato

A technique used by string players in which the string is plucked rather than bowed to create a light, percussive sound. Abbreviated *pizz.*

Plagal cadence

The progression of **chords** IV to I at the end of a musical phrase, creating a feeling of completion. Also called *amen cadence.*

| IV | I |
| F | C |

Plainsong

An ancient type of unison vocal music dating back to early Christian times, and still used today during Roman Catholic services.

Polyphony

The combination of interweaving melodies. See also **counterpoint.**

Portamento

An effect used to glide from one pitch to another so that intermediate **microtones**

are briefly sounded. This effect is only possible on instruments such as the violin, **fretless bass,** or **synthesizer.**

Power chord

A term used for a two-note guitar chord made up of the root and fifth. Usually the root is also doubled at a higher **octave.** Power chords are crucial to the rhythm parts of heavier **rock** styles.

Pre-amp

A type of amplifier used to condition and boost a weak signal to the point where it can be fed into a *power amp.* Most guitar amplifiers contain a built-in pre-amp which may be used to overdrive the power amp and produce *distortion.*

Presto

The fastest tempo, usually executed in a quick and sprightly manner.

Progressive rock

A musical style of the 1970s with an emphasis on virtuosity and experimentation in the recording studio. Progressive rock borrowed many elements from **classical** music (including the **concerto** and **opera** forms). Definitive albums in this style include *The Lamb Lies Down on Broadway* (Genesis, 1974), *Tales from Topographic Oceans* (Yes, 1974), and *Dark Side of the Moon* (Pink Floyd, 1973).

Punch-in

A recording technique used to correct
mistakes. The musician plays along with
the recorded part and the engineer starts
recording at the moment where the error
occurred. Once the musician has
supplied the correct notes, the engineer
cancels the record mode.

Punk rock

A style of **rock** music developed in the
1970s, punk is characterized by brevity,
harmonic simplicity, fast **tempos**,
aggresive delivery, and sneering,
chanted vocals. Definitive punk rock
albums include *Never Mind the Bollocks*
(Sex Pistols, 1977), *London Calling*
(The Clash, 1979), and *The Ramones*
(The Ramones, 1976).

Quadruplet

Four notes played in the time that it would normally take to play three of the same value. The quadruplet is to **compound time** what the **triplet** is to **simple time.**

Quantize

A process in MIDI sequencing that automatically corrects slight deviances in timing to produce a part that is perfectly in tempo.

Quartal harmony

A type of harmony featuring chord structures based on fourths rather than thirds.

Quarter note

A note with half the duration of a **half note.** In most circumstances, the quarter note lasts for one beat.

Quarter tone

An interval that is half the size of a half step. Quarter tones commonly occur in non-Western music, as well as some avant-garde classical and rock music. See also **microtone.**

R

Raga
A form of Indian music involving scale figures that are used as the basis for improvisation. Different ragas are associated with different moods and suitable times for performance.

Ragtime
A type of early **jazz** music developed in the early twentieth century. Ragtime is often characterized by inventive and lighthearted syncopation. This distinctive style of music is epitomized by the elegant piano compositions of Scott Joplin.

Rallentando
Gradually slow down the **tempo.** Abbreviated *rall.*

Rap
A musical genre popularized by African-American artists during the 1980s and 1990s. Here **melody** is replaced by a highly rhythmic delivery of rhymed, colloquial lyrics. This is accompanied by a driving beat from a **sampler** or **beatbox,** often with the addition of simple **synthesizer** parts and chanted backup vocals. See also **hip-hop.**

Rasguado
A strumming technique used by **flamenco** guitarists consisting of a rapid, sequential uncurling of the fingers to produce a sustained barrage of sound.

Real time
A term coined in the wake of the digital music revolution to describe a non-programmed musical performance recorded at the same tempo as it is played back.

Recapitulation
The restatement of a musical theme in a piece, typically a **sonata.**

Recitative
A form of singing resembling speech that is commonly used in opera to advance the plot. See also **aria** and **opera.**

Refrain
A repeating passage in a song that typically occurs after a **verse** or **bridge.** See also **chorus.**

Reggae
A popular musical style that evolved in the 1960s from traditional Jamaican **folk music** as influenced by **soul** and **rhythm and blues.** Reggae music is characterized by electronic instrumentation, simple harmonic changes, and pronounced **offbeats.** The lyrics often express ideas and beliefs central to Rastafarianism. Reggae music

gained international attention through the work of Bob Marley and the Wailers in the 1970s.

Relative key
A major key and a minor key that share the same key signature are said to be relative keys. For example, G is the *relative major* of E Minor because both keys share the key signature of one sharp. By the same token, E Minor is the *relative minor* of G.

Resolution
A general term for the release of tension in music caused when a **dissonance** changes to a **consonance**.

Rest
A symbol used to indicate a period of silence. Every note has an corresponding rest of equivalent duration. Adding a dot after a rest increases its length by one-half.

	dotted
eighth- = ¹/₂ beat	quarter- = 1 ¹/₂ beats
note rest	note rest

Reverb
1. Short for *reverberation*, this term describes the natural **acoustic** properties of a performance space.
2. An electronic effect that adds a lively quality to a recording or performance. Different styles of popular music are characterized by different types of

reverb. For example, during the 1980s, reverb was typically used to enhance drum parts. The producers of the 1990s tend to favor a drum sound that is less **wet.**

Rhapsody
An instrumental piece of medium length with an informal structure and a romantic, fantastical character, often inpsired by **folk music**. The rhapsody was popularized in the nineteenth century by composers such as Chopin and Liszt. This whimsical form is also favored by modern composers such as George Gershwin and Vaughan Williams.

Rhythm
A term used to describe elements of timing and accentuation in a musical composition. Rhythm comprises the **tempo**, type of beat, number of beats in a **bar,** and the rhythm patterns generated by the note values and accents employed by different instruments and voices.

Rhythm and blues
A popular African-American music developed in the 1940s as an outgrowth of **blues** and gospel music. As its name implies, rhythm and blues has a prominent **rhythm,** and an earthy, blues-influenced tone. Sometimes abbreviated *R&B*, this appealing musical style influenced the Beatles, the Rolling Stones, the Who, and other early **rock**

bands. R&B itself persisted as a musical genre during the 1960s and 1970s, but was then largely replaced by soul. Today some soul and dance music is still described as rhythm and blues.

Riff
A colloquial expression for a short musical phrase used as a building block in instrumental arrangements of **jazz, rock,** and pop music. Riffs are often repeated in variations throughout a song, especially when the melody line is at rest. Also called a *lick*.

Risoluto
A musical direction indicating the performer should play in a resolute or bold manner.

Rock
A popular music form developed from a mixture of country, **blues,** and **rhythm and blues.** In the 1950s, rock music was popularized by Elvis Presley, Little Richard, and Chuck Berry. During the 1960s, the form was further developed by the Beatles, the Rolling Stones, the Who, and many others. Like pop, rock music features songs of three to four minutes that are characterized by extensive repetition, simple harmonies, and a steady ⁴⁄₄ beat.

Rockabilly
A blend of country and **rock** music, rockabilly was popularized in the 1950s. Originally, the rockabilly band typically featured acoustic guitars and double bass. Rockabilly was pioneered by such artists as Carl Perkins and Elvis Presley. Rockabilly was revived in the 1980s by the Stray Cats and Robert Gordon.

Romantic
European music of the nineteenth century characterized by the emotional expression of dramatic and picturesque themes in a wide variety of forms.

Rondo
An instrumental composition in which the initial section is followed by a new contrasting section. This sequence is then repeated one or more times (*e.g.,* ABACADA).

Root position
A term used to describe a **chord** in which the lowest note is the **tonic** note. See **inversion.**

Round
A **canon** for several voices in **unison,** with each voice beginning at a different time. Usually performed without accompaniment. See **a capella** and **catch.**

Rubato
A musical direction indicating the performer should play or sing the marked passage freely. Rubato passages are typically used to add an emotional quality to a piece.

S

Sampler
An electronic device popularized in the mid 1980s that records and stores sounds in a format that can then be manipulated using a MIDI keyboard or computer **sequencer.**

Sarabande
An instrumental dance of the sixteenth century that later became the third movement of a **suite.**

Scale
A linear arrangement of notes from which a sense of **key** and **harmony** may be derived. Scale forms include the **major scale, minor scale, whole-tone scale,** and scales of various **modes.**

Scat singing
An improvisational singing style used in **jazz** music that employs nonsense syllables to evoke the quality of an instrumental solo. This style was introduced by Louis Armstrong and Cab Calloway in the 1920s, and further developed in the next decades by Ella Fitzgerald, among others.

Semi-acoustic
A term used to describe a type of hollow-bodied guitar that is fitted with electronic **pickups,** but also able to produce some **acoustic** sound. Semi-acoustic guitars are favored by **jazz** musicians.

Semitone
See **half step.**

Sequencer
A type of computer software or standalone device that allows a series of MIDI commands to be recorded, edited, and played back as a musical piece.

Serenade
A love song originally sung outside the window of a beloved at evening. During the late eighteenth century, this term was applied to instrumental music in the style of a love song.

Sharp
A sign placed in front of a note, raising it by a **half step.** A type of **accidental.** See also **flat** and **natural.**

Sightreading
Playing or singing written music at first sight.

Simple time
A **time signature** in which each pulse consists of a single note or its equivalent (*e.g.,* $\frac{2}{4}$, $\frac{3}{4}$, or $\frac{4}{4}$). See also **compound time.**

Sitar
An Indian lute with a long neck, usually played with a **pick.**

Sixteenth note
A note with half the duration of an **eighth note.** In most circumstances, the sixteenth note lasts for one-quarter of a beat.

Skiffle
An African-American song form originated in the 1930s, skiffle features songs of three or four **chords** traditionally played on folk instruments such as the guitar, harmonica, and washtub bass. Skiffle was an influence on artists of the late 1950s and early 1960s including the Beatles and Lonnie Donegan.

Slapback
A type of echo effect devised in the 1950s featuring a single repeated note after the original note. Slapback may be heard on many of the early Sun recordings of Elvis Presley.

Slide
A playing technique that involves a **slur** from one note to another. A guitar slide is accomplished by striking a string, then sliding the fretting finger (or slide device) up or down the string to create a smooth movement from one note to another. See also **bottleneck** and **glissando.**

Slur
A playing technique whereby the player moves from one note to another without articulating the second note. See also **slide** and **glissando.**

Snare
A small drum with a treble quality, the snare is an essential part of the contemporary drum kit. See **bass drum.**

Sonata
A musical piece presented in three or four contrasting sections, usually featuring a solo instrument.

Song cycle
A compositional form developed by Franz Schubert during the nineteenth century in which several songs are combined to create a single work.

Soprano
A female vocal range, spanning from **Middle C** to G above the treble staff.

Soul music
A style of African-American music originating in the 1960s as an outgrowth of **blues, rhythm and blues,** and **gospel** music. Soul music is characterized by syncopated rhythms and a declamatory vocal style with extensive vocal ornaments. This musical style was originally produced on the **Motown,**

Atlantic, and Stax record labels, and is still produced today.

Soundcheck
A run-through before a live concert to test that the sound systems are functioning properly so that the sound technicians can get a good mix.

Staccato
A lightly accented note of short duration indicated by a dot above or beneath the note head.

Staff
In standard music notation, an arrangement of five lines on which music is written. The type of **clef** used determines which pitches are indicated by notes on the lines and spaces of the staff.

Standard tuning
The customary tuning of a stringed instrument. For example, the standard guitar tuning is: E A D G B E. See also **open tuning.**

Stepwise motion
Progression by **half step** or **whole step,** usually in a melodic line.

Stratocaster
A type of **electric guitar** first produced in the 1950s by legendary guitar maker

Leo Fender. Also called a *Strat,* this instrument features three single-coil **pickups,** a five-way selector switch, and a tremolo arm. The so-called *superstrat* of the 1980s was produced by other guitar makers in imitation of this commercially successful guitar.

String quartet
An instrumental ensemble consisting of four string instruments: two violins, a viola, and a cello. Also, a work written for this instrumentation.

Subdominant
The fourth note and **chord** of the **scale.**

Subdominant (F)

Submediant
The sixth note and **chord** of the **scale.**

Submediant (A)

Suite
An instrumental form of the seventeenth and eighteenth centuries featuring dances in various movements typically including the **allemande,** courante, gigue, **minuet,** and **sarabande**.

Supertonic
The second note and **chord** of the **scale.**

Supertonic (D)

Suspension
A harmonic effect in which a chord is played with a **dissonant** note moving to a **consonance.** The most common occurrences are the *suspended fourth* and *suspended second chords*. This effect is frequently used in **folk** and pop music to create harmonic tension and interest.

Swing
A style of **jazz** music popular in the 1930s characterized by sophisticated arrangements with improvised solos. Swing music is usually performed by an instrumental combo or *big band*.

Sympathetic resonance
A sound that is produced by an unplayed string resulting from vibrations made when other strings are played.

Symphony
A large-scale work for **orchestra** in four movements.

Syncopation
A rhythmic effect created by emphasizing the **offbeats** of a composition or arrangement.

Synthesizer
An electronic instrument developed in the 1960s that generates a wide variety of sounds and wave forms. Typically a keyboard instrument, the synthesizer is important in almost every category of popular music today.

T

Tabla
A small Indian drum that is tuned to different pitches, and typically used to accompany the **sitar.**

Tablature
A system of music notation for a particular fretted instrument, often used in conjunction with standard music notation. In guitar tablature, six lines represent the six strings of the guitar, with the fret number for each note provided on the appropriate line.

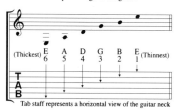

Open strings of the guitar

(Thickest) E A D G B E (Thinnest)
6 5 4 3 2 1

Tab staff represents a horizontal view of the guitar neck

Example of notation and TAB

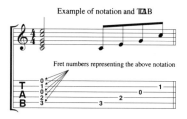

Fret numbers representing the above notation

Tapping
A playing technique popularized in the late 1970s by electric guitarist Eddie Van Halen. Tapping was a mainstay in the **hard rock** of the 1980s, as exemplified in the playing of Steve Vai and Joe Satriani. Rather than picking, the guitarist sounds notes by "tapping" notes along one string with fingers of both hands. This allows for the execution of very swift and smooth **arpeggios.**

Techno
A dance music popularized in the 1990s that is characterized by rapid **tempos,** simple **harmony,** and **synthesized** sound.

Temperament
A system of tuning in which **enharmonic** tones (*e.g.,* C♯ and D♭) are slightly raised or lowered to make them sound more perfectly in tune.

Tempo
The rate of speed at which a musical composition is played, often indicated by a *tempo marking.* See also **a tempo, accelerando, adagio, andante, allegro, BPM, giusto, largo, moderato, presto, rallentando, real time,** and **rubato.**

Tenor
A high male vocal range, spanning from D below **Middle C** to the G above it. Music for tenor voice is usually written one **octave** higher than it sounds using the treble **clef.**

Tenuto
A note held for its full value (or slightly longer), indicated by a short line above or beneath the note head.

Ternary form
A musical form with three complementary sections, usually A-B-A.

Tetrachord
A series of four stepwise notes spanning the **interval** of a perfect fourth. The major scale consists of two tetrachords separated by a **whole step,** each with this interval sequence: whole step, whole step, half step.

Theremin
The first electronic instrument, developed in Russia during the 1920s by Leon Theremin. Equipped with a radio receiver and antenna, the Theremin is played using hand movements. This rare instrument was improved in the 1960s by Robert Moog and may be heard on the Beach Boys' "Good Vibrations."

Threshold
A control typically found on compressors, **noise gates,** and **enhancers.** Setting the threshold specifies the volume level at which a sound processing effect will switch on.

Tie
A curved line that connects two notes of the same pitch indicating that they be played as one tone with a duration equal to their combined time value.

Tierce de Picardie
The use of a major chord at the end of a composition or movement in a minor key; common in music of the eighteenth century. Also called *Picardy third.*

Timbre
The tonal quality of a voice or instrument.

Time code
A form of digital data embedded in a recording; used to synchronize digital instruments, **sequencers,** or recording devices.

Time signature
A symbol after the **clef** at the beginning of a piece indicating the metre to be used. Usually shown as two numbers, with the top number indicating the overall number of beats in each **bar** and the lower number showing the type of beat used.

three quarter-note beats in a bar   six eighth-note beats in a bar

Toccata
An early composition for keyboard with a rapid, flowing style, typically including scalar themes and bold **counterpoint.**

Tone
1. A note or pitch.
2. The **timbre** of an instrument or voice.

Tone poem
An orchestral form that portrays the themes of a story or poem in one movement. This form was favored by **Romantic** composers such as Richard Strauss and Edward Elgar. Also known as a *symphonic poem.*

Tone row
See **twelve-tone music.**

Tonic
The first note and **chord** of the **scale.**

Tonic minor
The minor **key** built on the same **tonic** note as a given major key.

Transposition
A musical composition that has been changed to a different key (usually without any other significant alterations).

Transposing instrument
An instrument that is notated in a key different from the one actually played. The alto saxophone, for example, sounds in E♭ when it is notated a major sixth higher in the key of C. This convention makes it easier to read and write music, as the main range of the instrument falls within the treble **staff.** Most brass and woodwind instruments are transposing instruments.

E♭ alto saxophone sounds a major sixth below the written pitch. Rule: **Written C sounds E♭**

Written

Sounds

French Horn

Saxophone

Tremolo

1. For stringed instruments, the repetition of a note using short rapid movements of a bow or **pick.**
2. For keyboard instruments, the rapid alteration of two notes.
3. An effect available on early guitar amps that varies the volume of the sound in a cyclical manner.

Triad

A **chord** with three notes, usually the root, third, and fifth of the

corresponding **scale**. There are four basic forms: major triad (C E G), minor triad (C E♭ G), **augmented** triad (C E G♯), and **diminished** triad (C E♭ G♭).

Trio

1. An ensemble consisting of three instrumentalists or singers.
2. A musical composition for three instrumentalists or vocalists.
3. A composition in three movements, usually in **sonata** form.
4. The middle section of a minuet or march, usually a contrasting dance or march.

Triplet

Three equal notes played in the time of two, typically indicated by the numeral *3*. The triplet evokes the skipping **rhythm** of compound time when in **simple time.**

Tritone

Two notes that are three whole-steps apart, forming the interval of an augmented fourth (or flatted fifth). The use of this interval was forbidden in Medieval times because it was associated with the Devil. The tritone's dark, discordant sound is frequently heard in **heavy metal** music.

Truss rod

A metal rod that runs through the neck of most steel-string guitars and that may be adjusted to correct certain intonation problems and warping.

Tube amp

A type of amplifier that uses vacuum tube technology. Popular in the 1960s, today the tube amp has largely been replaced by solid-state transistor amps, and hybrid amps which use both tube and solid-state technology.

Twelve-bar blues

A common form of **blues** consisting of three four-bar lines. Typically, the harmony progresses in this sequence: four bars of the I chord, followed by two bars of the IV chord, followed by another two bars of the I chord. The final four bars follow this sequence: V-IV-I-V.

Twelve-tone music

An atonal system devised by Schoenberg in the early twentieth century. **Keys** and **scales** are replaced with permutations of a series of twelve tones.

Twin neck

A type of guitar, usually electric, that has two necks attached to its body. Typically, one neck has six strings, while the other has twelve. This configuration is used in the Gibson ES-1275D which is associated with Jimmy Page of Led Zeppelin and John McLaughlin of the Mahavishnu Orchestra. Also called **doubleneck.**

U

Ukulele
A small fretted instrument popularized in the 1930s, originally related to the four-string Hawaiian guitar.

Una corda
A direction to a pianist indicating the left (soft) pedal should be depressed to create a muted effect. This causes the hammers to only strike one string per note played (instead of three). This direction is cancelled by the phrase *tre corda*.

Unequal voices
Another term for mixed voices, usually both male and female.

Unison
1. Notes of the same pitch.
2. Two or more instruments or voices performing at the same pitch are said to be *in unison*.

Unison bend
An electric guitar technique used to thicken phrases in **lead guitar** solos. Here one string is fretted, while a lower string is bent to the same pitch.

Upbeat
The unstressed beat that comes at the end of a bar. See also **anacrusis, downbeat,** and **offbeat.**

Vamp
A simple chordal introduction or interlude to a song, usually improvised.

Variation
The reiteration of a theme with altered harmonic, melodic, or rhythmic elements.

Verse
A section of a song, usually followed by a chorus or chorus, then typically repeated.

Vibrato
A subtle fluctuation in pitch produced by an instrumentalist or singer during a sustained note.

Viol
A bowed string instrument of the sixteenth century; the predecessor of the modern **violin.**

Violin
A small-bodied stringed instrument typically tuned in fifths and played with a bow.

Viola
A stringed instrument similar to the **violin,** but tuned a fifth lower to produce deeper tones.

Virtuoso
A vocalist or instrumentalist with a high degree of proficiency.

Voicing
The choice of notes for a given **chord.** A simple **triad** has three notes, but these could be arranged in a number of different ways. These possibilities are known as voicings.

W

Wah-wah

A foot-operated effects pedal used by **electric guitarists** to alter the **tone** enabling them to produce sounds resembling vocal effects.

Walking bass

A bass style found in **jazz** and some **rock** music that involves repeated scalar bass figures.

Wall of sound

An arrangement style pioneered by record producer Phil Spector in the 1960s characterized by full arrangements that create thick sonic textures.

Waltz

A form of dance in ¾ time popularized in the nineteenth century.

West Coast jazz

A style of restrained improvisational **jazz** popular during the 1950s. West Coast jazz is exemplified in the work of Chet Baker and Dave Brubeck.

West Coast rock

A style of **rock** music popular from about 1966 to 1975. It often features harmonized vocals and a free-spirited, breezy open feel. Influential groups include the Byrds, Jefferson Airplane, and the Eagles.

Wet

A term used to describe a sound signal laden with effects processing (particularly **reverb**). Opposite of **dry.**

Whammy bar

A device that attaches to the tailpiece of an **electric guitar** and allows the tension of the strings to be easily lessened and increased to create a **vibrato** effect. Also called a *tremolo bar, tremolo arm,* or *vibrato bar.*

White noise

A sound comprising random electrically generated frequencies that create a steady background of static.

White notes

Notes played using the seven white keys of the **piano:** C D E F G A B.

Whole note

A note that lasts for a complete bar in ¾ or ⁴⁄₄ time.

Whole step
An **interval** comprising two **half-steps.**
Also called a **major second** or **tone.**

Whole-tone scale
A **scale** consisting of six notes
extending over an **octave** with a whole
step interval between each note. For
example, a whole-tone scale starting on
C is. C D E F♯ G♯ A♯ C.

Wolf note
A note on the guitar rendered weaker by
acoustic idiosyncrasies of that particular
instrument.

Word painting
A songwriting technique whereby the
music reflects the meaning of the lyrics.
For example, in Jim Webb's famous
song "Up, Up and Away" the melody
line ascends to reflect the words.

Xylophone
A percussion instrument consisting of
bars of wood of different lengths that
are tuned to graduated pitches. These
are struck with mallets to produce
pitched percussive tones.

Yodel
A singing technique associated with
Alpine folk songs and American
cowboy songs featuring rapid
fluctuations between the normal voice
and **falsetto.**

Zither
An instrument associated with the folk
music of Austria and Bavaria. The
modern zither has thirty-two strings,
five of which are strung across a
fretboard and used to play melodies.
The rest are used to play chords or to
create **sympathetic resonances.** See
also **koto.**